Guitar for Kids

How to Play, Master the Basics, and Jam Like a Rockstar

Table of Contents

Introduction

Have you ever heard a song so awesome it makes your feet stomp and your head bop? Have you ever wished you could play it, become a guitar superhero, and wow everyone with your epic skills? Buckle up because "Guitar for Kids" is your backstage pass to rock stardom.

Forget boring music books with confusing notes and dusty pages. This book isn't your grandma's guitar guide. It's your ultimate music adventure, packed with:

- **Secret Tricks to Mastering the Fretboard:** No more mind-bending scales or cryptic chords. It's broken down like a pizza (everyone loves pizza, right?), making every step clear and cheesy good.

- **Super-Fun Songs You'll Want to Play:** Ditch the lullabies and nursery rhymes. You'll be playing pop hits, movie themes, and maybe a pirate shanty or two (arrr, mateys).

- **Action-Packed Games and Challenges:** Learning shouldn't feel like homework. So, get ready for guitar quests, finger-twisting battles, and epic jam sessions that'll turn practice into playtime.

- **Cool Tips and Tricks to Impress Your Friends:** Learn how to bend strings like a rock legend, strum faster than a cheetah on Red Bull, and invent mind-blowing riffs.

Hold on, there's more. Unlike other books that treat you like a tiny music robot, "Guitar for Kids" gets you. It knows attention spans can be shorter than a goldfish's memory, so it keeps things short, sweet, and straight to the point. No long, boring lectures, only pure, unadulterated musical fun.

Plus, every rockstar is unique. So, whether you're a finger-picking princess, a headbanging hero, or a melody-making maestro, "Guitar for Kids" will meet you wherever you are and help unleash your inner guitar god (or goddess).

What are you waiting for? Grab your axe (that's guitar talk for your guitar), crack open "Guitar for Kids," and get ready to rock your world. Remember, every legendary musician started somewhere, and that somewhere could be right here, right now, with you.

So, crank up the volume, let the music take over, and become the guitar hero you were always meant to be. The stage is waiting, and the spotlight is on you.

Are you ready to rock? Turn the page and let the adventure begin.

Chapter 1: Introduction to Guitars

Have you ever heard a song so powerful it makes your heartbeat like a drum and your feet tap a silent rhythm? Have you ever dreamed of wielding that magic, of conjuring emotions from wooden strings and vibrating air? Welcome to the world of the guitar, an instrument as old as stories themselves. It's a companion to kings and rebels and a voice that can sing lullabies and scream anthems.

1. Welcome to the world of the guitar, an instrument as old as stories themselves. Source: https://www.pexels.com/photo/boy-in-gray-cardigan-sitting-on-brown-leather-couch-playing-guitar-7520794/

This chapter is your first step into its enchanted realm, where you unravel its secrets, from the curves of its body to the coolness of its strings. Prepare to meet your musical companion, a gateway to a universe of sonic expression waiting to be explored.

The Anatomy of a Musical Marvel

Music speaks a language understood by all, and string instruments sing their enchanting tales. However, have you ever wondered about the mechanics behind their melodious magic? It's time to dive into the captivating anatomy of a string instrument, exploring the differences between plucked and bowed beauties, tuning systems, and the evolution of the iconic six-string configuration.

- **Plucked vs. Bowed:** Plucked instruments like the guitar, harp, and banjo tremble under direct contact, creating a percussive, intimate sound. In contrast, bowed instruments like the violin, cello, and viola rely on a horsehair bow gliding across the strings, coaxing out a smooth, sustained tone. It's a difference in touch, a conversation between instrument and player, with each method yielding a unique sonic fingerprint.

- **The E-A-D-G-B-E Enigma:** The six-string guitar might be a common sight, but its history and tuning hold fascinating secrets. The iconic E-A-D-G-B-E arrangement, known as standard tuning, wasn't always set in stone. Centuries of experimentation led to this configuration, optimized for playing chords and melodies effortlessly. Like a passionate character, each open string contributes its voice to the symphony of sound. Guitars are chameleons, capable of adopting alternate tunings to unlock new sonic doors, each variation singing a different musical story.

- **Electric vs. Acoustic:** With its resonant body and air-driven vibrations, the acoustic guitar is a timeless storyteller. Its warmth and intimacy have enchanted audiences for centuries. Then came the electric revolution, amplifying the instrument's voice and propelling it into the realms of rock and roll. Electric guitars, armed with pickups and amplifiers, transformed sound, bending notes, adding distortion, and unleashing sonic storms. Yet, acoustic, and electric instruments, despite their differences, share a common soul. Their strings vibrate with the player's passion, weaving music medleys through wood, wire, and air.

The Guitar's Cultural Pilgrimage

The guitar, a seemingly simple instrument of wood and strings, holds a universe of cultural narratives within its frets and resonance box. Its journey across continents and genres comprises diverse voices, social movements, and political expressions. The guitar can transcend boundaries, ignite revolutions, and symbolize hope and resistance.

- **A Global Nomad:** From the blues-soaked deltas of the Mississippi to the fiery flamenco of Spain, the guitar has traversed oceans and continents, adapting to local rhythms and traditions. The six-stringed instrument donned the poncho of the mariachi in Mexico, the kora skin in West Africa, and the sitar's silken strings in India. Each iteration is a testament to the instrument's remarkable ability to absorb and transform, becoming a mirror reflecting the soul of its adopted home.

- **A Catalyst for Change:** The guitar's voice has been a potent weapon in the fight for social justice and political change. From the protest songs of Woody Guthrie and Joan Baez during the Civil Rights movement to the anthems of Chilean resistance against Pinochet's dictatorship, the instrument has amplified the voices of the marginalized and given voice to the voiceless. Its chords have echoed through student protests, resonated in the chants of workers' unions, and been a soundtrack to countless revolutions, reminding people that music can be a powerful tool for change.

- **A Symbol of Many Meanings:** In diverse cultures, the guitar transcends its physical form to become a potent symbol. In flamenco, it embodies fiery passion and the spirit of Andalusia. In blues, it speaks of hardship and resilience. Its mournful notes are a testament to the African American experience. In rock and roll, it becomes a symbol of rebellion and youth, an amplified roar of challenge to societal norms. The guitar's multifaceted symbolism highlights its ability to speak to the human condition in many ways, resonating with the hopes, dreams, and struggles of people across the globe.

The Guitar's Many Musical Faces

With its six versatile strings and boundless potential, the guitar is an instrument not only for playing but also for speaking. It's a chameleon, adapting to a multitude of musical landscapes. Each genre is a platform for your unique voice to shine. Buckle up, aspiring musician, because you're on a sonic journey, exploring the diverse ways the guitar sings.

- **Classical Grace:** Picture yourself bathed in the warm glow of a concert hall, fingers gliding across the fretboard, weaving Bach's intricate melodies or Tárrega's passionate flamenco rhythms. With its focus on technical precision and melodic beauty, the classical guitar demands dedication and refinement. But, oh, the rewards. Mastering this style unlocks a world of elegance and musical depth, where each note becomes a brushstroke on a sonic canvas.

- **Rock and Roll Rebellion:** Crank up the amp, let the distortion rip, and unleash your inner rockstar. The guitar is the heart and soul of rock. Its crunchy power chords and soaring solos define the genre. From Hendrix's psychedelic riffs to Slash's bluesy fury, rock guitar offers a playground for experimentation and raw expression. Whether you shred like a speed demon or groove like a seasoned bluesman, your guitar amplifies your rebellious spirit.

- **Jazz's Melodic Playground:** Step into a smoky nightclub where improvisation reigns supreme, and every note is a conversation. The jazz guitar's focus is on harmony, improvisation, and rhythmic complexity, and demands a deep understanding of music theory and a willingness to take risks. For the adventurous soul, the freedom and creativity offered by jazz are unparalleled. Let your fingers dance across the fretboard, creating counterpoint melodies and unexpected chords, and join the endless jazz improvisation conversation.

- **Folk's Heartfelt Stories:** Gather around the campfire, strumming chords that speak tales of love, loss, and the natural world's beauty. The folk guitar, emphasizing storytelling and simple yet evocative melodies, is an instrument for the soul. Whether you fingerpick Dylan's timeless classics or strum to traditional Irish jigs, your guitar becomes a bridge between generations, carrying the echoes of countless stories through time.

- **Solo and Jamming:** The guitar's magic extends beyond individual genres. It's an instrument of collaboration where you join forces with other musicians. It's a tool for solo expression, where your unique voice takes center stage, painting sonic landscapes with every note. It's an invitation to improvisation, where you break free from the score and let your musical instincts guide you, creating melodies that dance on the edge of the unknown.

Now, you've glimpsed the magic held within a guitar's soul. However, knowledge, like a seed, is only the beginning. To turn it into music, you'll need practice, patience, and, most of all, passion. Let your fingers become storytellers. Don't be afraid to stumble because every wrong note is a steppingstone to mastery. The greatest melody starts with a single note, and the music within you is waiting to be heard.

Chapter 2: Getting Started with the Guitar

Welcome, dear aspiring musician, to the first chord of your guitar adventure. This chapter is your roadmap to unlocking the magic of this six-stringed friend. You'll dive into choosing the perfect instrument, dissecting its anatomy, and establishing a comfortable foundation for posture and hand positioning. All these are essential ingredients for your journey to musical mastery. So, grab a pick and tune in because it's time to get strumming.

2. Prepare to dive into choosing the perfect instrument. Source: https://www.pexels.com/photo/focused-black-girl-taking-notes-on-paper-6437589/

Finding the Perfect Match

Picking your first guitar is like finding a long-lost friend. It should feel just right. However, with so many options available, choosing one might feel like navigating a complex melody. It's time to break down the process like a simple blues riff.

- **Budget:** First things first, set a realistic budget. Remember, you don't need a platinum-plated axe to start. It's like buying your first pair of sneakers.

You wouldn't break the bank on a fancy pair for running practice, right? While budget guitars might not have all the bells and whistles, they are still fantastic learning companions. Aim for a decent beginner instrument in the $100-$500 range. It's an investment in your musical journey, not a splurge on a luxury item.

- **Size Matters:** Guitars come in various sizes, and like Goldilocks, finding the right fit is crucial. For adults, a standard-sized guitar (around 41 inches) is ideal. Younger players will find "three-quarter" or "half" sizes more comfortable and manageable. A guitar that feels like a miniature giant will only frustrate you and hinder your progress.

- **Playing Style:** What music do you hear echoing in your soul? Gentlefolk ballads or electrifying rock anthems? Each genre thrives on specific guitar types. Acoustic guitars, with their natural, wood-toned voice, are perfect for folk, country, and singer-songwriter styles. Electric guitars, with their amp-powered versatility, can tackle rock, blues, metal, and anything in between. Choose an instrument that speaks to the music you want to create, not the music someone else tells you to play.

- **Tone Preference:** Close your eyes and imagine your ideal guitar sound. Warm and mellow like a crackling fireplace? Bright and crisp like a summer breeze? Different woods affect the tone, just like different spices add flavor to a dish. Spruce tops are brighter, like a zesty lemon, while mahogany leans toward warmth, like a comforting cup of cocoa. Research popular tonewoods and listen to guitars online to get a feel for what speaks to your ears. Remember, the tone is a personal fingerprint. Find one that resonates with you.

- **Testing Is Key:** Don't buy a guitar online. It's like buying shoes without trying them on. You might end up with something uncomfortable and unusable. Visit a music store, ask questions, and, most importantly, try out different guitars. See which feels comfortable in your hands, like a well-worn pair of gloves. Feel the weight, the neck thickness, and the overall balance. Find the one that speaks to your soul with its sound, like a song that makes your heart skip a beat. Trust your gut feeling. The right guitar will sing to you, not just sit on a shelf gathering dust.

- **Brand Buzz:** While brand names can be alluring, don't let them be the sole deciding factor. It's like choosing a restaurant based on its fancy name, not the food quality. Focus on features, sound, and feel. However, beginner-friendly brands like Yamaha, Fender, and Epiphone are known for their quality and affordability. A good brand is just the first chord, not the whole song.

Choosing your first guitar is an exciting step, not a final destination. You might upgrade or add different instruments to your musical family as you progress. For now, find one that sparks your excitement and gets you playing. Don't get caught up in the pressure of finding the "perfect" one. Sometimes, the best guitar is the one that gets you started on your musical journey.

Understanding the Basic Parts of the Guitar

Learning to play the guitar is an exciting journey, and it all begins with understanding the instrument. Don't let its six-stringed splendor intimidate you. This section dismantles it piece by piece, transforming it from a complex puzzle into a roadmap for your musical adventure.

Breakdown of the Headstock, Neck, Fretboard, Body, and Hardware

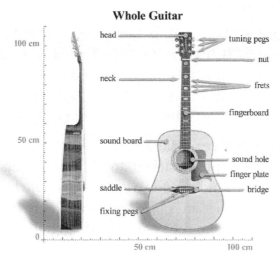

3. Acoustic guitar anatomy. Source: Dominic Alves, CC BY 2.0 <https://creativecommons.org/licenses/by/2.0>, via Wikimedia Commons. https://commons.wikimedia.org/wiki/File:Acoustic_Guitar_Anatomy.jpg

1. **Headstock:** The headstock is at the top of the guitar. It holds the tuning pegs or tuners, which are crucial for adjusting the strings' tension. The strings are wound around these pegs, allowing you to tune your guitar to the desired pitch.

2. **Neck:** The neck is the long, slender part of the guitar that extends from the body and connects to the headstock. It contains the frets, which are metal strips embedded along the fretboard. Frets help you create different notes by pressing down on the strings against them.

3. **Fretboard:** The fretboard is the flat, usually wooden surface on the front side of the neck. It's where you place your fingers to change the pitch of the notes produced by the strings. Fretboards often have markers to help you identify specific frets quickly.

4. **Body:** The body is the larger, curvier part of the guitar. It houses the sound hole(s) in an acoustic guitar or the pickups in an electric guitar. The body contributes to the guitar's resonance and tone, making it an integral part of the instrument.

5. **Hardware:** Hardware refers to the various components attached to the guitar, such as the bridge, saddle, and strap buttons. The bridge holds the strings in place, the saddle helps transmit vibrations to the body, and strap buttons allow you to attach a strap for comfortable playing.

Understanding Strings, Tuners, Pickups, and Controls

Understanding these foundational components provides a solid foundation for anyone embarking on their guitar-playing journey. It's time to explore the guitar's functionality specifics.

1. **Strings:** Guitars typically have six strings, each tuned to a specific pitch. The thickest string is the low E, and the thinnest is the high E. The notes produced by the strings can be altered by pressing down on different frets along the fretboard.

2. **Tuners:** On the headstock, tuners allow you to adjust the tension of each string. Turning the tuners clockwise or counterclockwise changes the pitch of the corresponding string. Regularly tuning your guitar ensures it always sounds its best.

3. **Pickups:** Electric guitars have pickups and small devices on the body under the strings. Pickups convert the vibrations of the strings into electrical signals, which are then amplified to produce sound. Different pickups will create distinct tones.

4. **Controls:** Electric guitars often have control knobs on the body to adjust the volume and tone. These controls help you tailor your sound to suit your preferences. Experimenting with different settings leads to unique and personalized tones.

Naming and Identifying Accessories like Picks, Straps, and Capos

Now that you're familiar with the strings, tuners, pickups, and controls, you're well on your way to unlocking the full potential of your guitar. However, there's more to explore. Here are some accessories that will enhance your playing experience.

1. **Picks:** Picks, or plectrums, are small, flat pieces usually made of plastic. They pluck or strum the

strings. Picks come in various shapes and thicknesses, enabling you to experiment with different tones and playing styles.

2. **Straps:** Guitar straps attach to the strap buttons on the body so you can play your guitar while standing. Straps provide comfort and stability, especially during longer playing sessions or live performances.

3. **Capos:** A capo is a device placed across the fretboard to change the pitch of the strings. It allows you to play in different keys without changing your finger positions. Capos are handy for exploring various musical styles and adapting songs to your vocal range.

As you explore guitar playing, don't forget about the accessories. Picks, straps, and capos may seem like small additions, but they significantly enhance your playing experience and open up new possibilities in your musical journey. Understanding the essential parts of the guitar and the associated accessories is fundamental for aspiring guitarists. Armed with this knowledge, you're well-equipped to navigate the exciting path of learning and creating music on this versatile instrument.

Posture and Hand Positioning for Guitar Newbies

But hold on, aspiring guitar hero. Before you launch into your first power chord, you must understand the importance of posture and hand positioning. These might sound like boring details, but they're the foundation for preventing injuries and rocking out pain-free for years.

4. *Proper posture. Source: https://www.pexels.com/photo/father-and-son-sitting-on-a-high-chair-while-playing-guitar-together-7520945/*

Posture: Sit Like a King, Play Like a Rock God

Your body is your guitar's support system. Slouching or hunching will make playing uncomfortable and limit your reach. Here's how to sit like a rockstar:

- **Chair Height:** Your feet must be flat on the floor, knees slightly bent. Your spine should make a straight line from your head to your tailbone.

- **Guitar Placement:** Rest the guitar body on your dominant leg, snuggled against your torso. The neck should angle slightly upwards, not pointing straight out.

- **Neck Grip:** Don't completely wrap your thumb around the neck's back. Instead, let it rest gently on the side, providing support without tension.

Fretting Hand: Building Finger Strength without Finger Pain

Your fretting hand becomes one with the guitar's neck, sliding up and down to create higher and lower pitches. Here are tips for smooth fretting:

- **Keep Your Wrist Straight:** Bend it too much, and you're asking for carpal tunnel. Your wrist should be an extension of your forearm, in line with the neck.

- **Fingertips, Not Claws:** Press down on the strings with the fleshy pads of your fingertips, not the nails. It ensures clear notes and avoids unnecessary strain.

- **Curve Your Fingers Slightly:** This natural curve helps you press down more evenly and comfortably.

Picking Hand: Unleashing Your Inner Master of String Manipulation

Your picking hand is your rhythm engine. Here's how to avoid fatigue and unlock your picking prowess:

- **Relaxed Grip:** Don't grip the pick like a life raft. Hold it loosely between your thumb and index finger, using just enough pressure to control it.

- **Wrist Movement:** For strumming, move your wrist, not your elbow. It keeps your hand relaxed and prevents tension.

- **Pick Angle:** Experiment with different angles to find your sweet spot. Generally, a 45-degree angle to the strings gives you a clear, bright sound.

Stretching and Warm-Up: Preventing Pain Before It Starts

Like athletes, guitarists need to warm up. Before you dive into your favorite riffs, do gentle stretches for your neck, shoulders, wrists, and fingers. Hold each stretch for 15-30 seconds and repeat 2-3 times.

Remember:

- **Start Slow and Build:** Don't push yourself too hard at first. Let your body adapt to the new movements gradually.

- **Listen to Your Body:** If you feel pain, stop immediately and rest. Pushing through pain will lead to injuries.

- **Practice Makes Perfect Posture:** The more you play with proper posture and hand positioning, the more natural it will feel.

So, there you have it, aspiring guitar hero, the secrets to pain free playing. By focusing on good posture and hand positioning, you'll be well on your way to shredding like a pro without the aches and pains holding you back.

Mastering the guitar isn't only about learning chords and riffs. It's about building a solid foundation by choosing the right gear, understanding its anatomy, and adopting perfect posture and finger positioning. When each element is in tune, the music flows effortlessly, and your journey from newbie to guitar hero becomes a joy, not a struggle. So, take your time, embrace the learning process, and remember, a well-prepared musician is a happy musician, ready to create and conquer.

Chapter 3: Guitar Playing Techniques

In the previous chapter, you explored the essence of the guitar, including its anatomy, gear, and posture. Now, it's time to truly speak its language and learn the alphabet of strokes and melodies that dance across its strings. This chapter is your initiation into guitar playing techniques, where basic strokes and finger placement become the building blocks of musical expression.

5. Master various techniques. Source: https://www.pexels.com/photo/woman-teaching-a-child-how-to-play-the-guitar-8190062/

In this chapter, you'll discover the secrets of confidently strumming and mastering tuning control. Most importantly, you'll develop a keen sense of pitch and tone, giving your music its unique voice. So, pick up your guitar, embrace the joy of exploration, and get ready to transform those frets into a canvas for your musical soul.

Foundation of Sound: Strokes and Fingering

Whether fresh off unwrapping your first axe or brushing the dust off an old six-string, laying a solid foundation in strokes and fingering is crucial for building your musical journey. This section is your trusty roadmap as you navigate down-strums, up-strums, alternating strokes, and fingerpicking fundamentals. Prepare to master chords and coordinate your hands for rhythmic success.

Strokes

Your pick becomes an extension of your musical voice, and learning proper strokes is where that voice finds its rhythm.

- **Down-Strum:** With a relaxed wrist, flick your pick downwards across the strings, aiming for a clean, full sound. Practice on individual strings first, then move to complete strums, focusing on consistency and even spacing.

- **Up-Strum:** Reverse the movement. Flick the pick upward, starting from the lowest string and aiming for a lighter, airier sound. Master down-strums first, then incorporate up-strums for a more dynamic rhythm.

- **Alternating Strokes:** This one takes practice. Alternate down and up strokes in a fluid motion, ensuring each string gets hit once per cycle. Start slowly, focusing on accuracy and clean transitions, then gradually increase the speed.

Fingerpicking

Fingerpicking allows you to play individual notes and weave intricate melodies. Experiment with different picking patterns and practice muting unused strings with your picking hand for a clean sound. Here are tips to get you rolling:

- **Pattern Play:** Explore different fingerpicking patterns like alternating thumb, Travis picking, or arpeggios to add rhythmic and textural variety to your melodies.

- **Muting Maestro:** Tame unwanted string noise by gently resting your picking hand on unused strings near the bridge. It adds clarity and focus to your melodies.

- **Dynamics and Nuance:** Don't be a one-volume wonder. Vary your picking pressure to create whispers, playful accents, and emotional swells in your playing.

- **Melodic Adventures:** Go beyond simple single notes. Experiment with legato phrasing, connecting notes smoothly, and double stops (playing two notes simultaneously) to craft richer and more expressive melodies.

- **Experimentation Playground:** Try fingerpicking different chords, voicings, and inversions to explore new harmonic possibilities and add depth to your music.

- **Practice Patience:** Mastering fingerpicking takes time and dedicated practice. Start slow, focus on accuracy, and clean picking, and gradually increase speed and complexity as you gain confidence.

- **Listen and Learn:** Immerse yourself in the playing of fingerstyle masters like Tommy Emmanuel, Andy McKee, or James Taylor. Watch, listen, and analyze their techniques to refine your style.

- **Beyond the Basics:** Once you're comfortable with core techniques, venture into advanced fingerpicking, like hybrid picking (combining fingerstyle and pick), cross-picking, and slapping techniques to expand your sonic palette.

Chords

Chords are the building blocks of harmony. Hence, learning a few basic chords opens a vast musical universe. Start with simple open chords, where all fingers press down on frets. Practice forming the chord shapes accurately and cleanly, focusing on finger independence and minimizing buzzing. It's time to add visual flair to your musical foundation by exploring a few essential chords and their finger positions.

Here are essential open chords to conquer:

- **E Major (E):** This bright, cheerful chord is your first stepping stone, the hero of countless songs. Place your index finger on the first fret of string G, your middle finger should be on the second fret of string A, and your ring finger on the second fret of string D. Perform all six strings simultaneously.

- **A Major (A):** First, place your index finger on string D's second fret. Place your middle and ring fingers on the second fret of strings B and G. This simple shift creates a warm, inviting A-major chord, perfect for strumming along to those feel-good tunes.

- **D Major (D):** Now, it's time to take a bigger leap. Move your first finger up to the second fret of the G string. Keep your second finger on the second fret of the high-E string and your third finger on the third fret of the B string. Strum only the bottom four strings for a bold, assertive D major chord, adding depth and power to your playing.

- **G Major (G):** This sunny chord shines with a bright, open sound. Put your first finger on the A string's second fret, your second finger on the low-E string's third fret, and your third finger on the high-E string's third fret. Now, play all strings together in harmony.

- **C Major (C):** This versatile chord adds a touch of warmth and stability to your music. Put your first finger on the B string's first fret, your second finger on the D string's second fret, and your third finger on the A string's third fret.

These five chords are just a taste of the vast chordal landscape waiting to be explored. As you get comfortable with them, experiment with other strumming patterns, fingerpicking techniques, and combining chords to create simple progressions.

Hand Coordination

Coordinating your fretting and picking hands is the magic behind creating rhythmic and melodic patterns. Start with simple strumming patterns while holding down a chord, ensuring each strum coincides with a change in the melody. Practice slowly, gradually increasing the speed and complexity as your coordination improves.

- **Patience Is Key:** Mastering these skills takes time and dedication. Celebrate small victories and be patient with yourself.

- **Practice Regularly:** Short, focused practice sessions are far more effective than sporadic bursts. Aim for 15-20 minutes daily, incorporating all the elements learned above.

- **Seek Guidance:** A good teacher will provide invaluable feedback and personalized techniques to accelerate your progress.

Building a solid foundation in strokes and fingering is like planting the seeds for a beautiful musical garden. With dedication and passion, you'll soon be harvesting the fruits of your labor, strumming your favorite tunes, and crafting your unique melodies.

Bonus Tip: Record yourself playing and listen to the playback. It'll help you identify areas for improvement and track your progress.

A Guitarist's Guide to Perfect Pitch

A versatile instrument with a voice that can whisper or roar, the guitar sings its truest song when in tune. However, achieving that perfect pitch isn't only about turning a knob.

It's a journey of understanding, a dance between technology and intuition, where the art of tuning becomes an essential skill for the guitarist.

Understanding Different Tunings

Standard tuning (E-A-D-G-B-E) is your trusty compass, the most widely used tuning for a reason. It offers familiarity, balance across the strings, and compatibility with the vast majority of songs and resources. However, the guitar's sonic palette extends far beyond standard. Explore some popular alternative tunings:

- **Drop D:** Lowering the E string a whole step to D (D-A-D-G-B-E) adds a deeper, heavier feel, perfect for blues and rock.

- **Open G:** Tuning all strings a whole step down to D-G-D-G-B-D creates a warm, resonant sound, ideal for fingerpicking and folk music.

- **Open E:** Tuning all strings down two whole steps to E-B-E-G#-B-E gives a unique, chiming sound favored by slide guitarists and blues players.

These are merely a few options. Experimenting with different tunings will spark new creative ideas and open avenues you never knew existed.

Tuning Tools

In the modern age, electronic tuners are your digital allies. They offer accuracy and versatility, often incorporating helpful features like built-in microphones and visual displays. Choose one that suits your needs and budget, and keep it handy for quick adjustments. Don't underestimate the power of the classic tuning fork. This simple, time-honored tool emits a specific pitch (usually A-440Hz) as a reference point for tuning your strings. While it might require practice and keen ears, using a tuning fork will develop your ear training and deepen your connection with the instrument's sound.

6. Tuning tools. Source: Boon Lee Fam, CC BY 2.0 <https://creativecommons.org/licenses/by/2.0>, via Wikimedia Commons. https://commons.wikimedia.org/wiki/File:Tool_Kit_for_Guitar_ Maintenance.jpg

Training Your Ear

Speaking of ear training, the ultimate goal is to tune your guitar by listening directly to the strings' vibrations. This skill takes time and dedication, but it offers immense benefits. Here are tips to get you started:

- **Start with Single Notes:** Isolate each string and compare its pitch to a reference point, like a tuning fork or an online tone generator. Learn to recognize the subtle differences in sound as you adjust the tuning pegs.

- **Tune in Harmony:** Once you can tune individual strings, practice tuning them in relation to each other. Learn the intervals between strings (for example, E to A is a perfect fifth) and use them as guideposts to achieve accurate tuning.

- **Listen to Music:** Pay close attention to how guitars are tuned in recordings and live performances. Identify the tuning used and analyze the characteristic sonic qualities it creates.

Ear training might feel daunting at first, but with consistent practice and patience, you'll gradually develop your aural acuity and become a master of tuning your guitar by sound. This skill empowers you to tune anywhere, anytime, and deepens your musical understanding and connection with your instrument.

Tuning is not a technical chore. It's the foundation upon which your musical expression rests. An in-tune guitar sings with clarity and confidence, allowing your melodies and chords to resonate with their full potential. So, embrace the art of tuning, explore different tunings, and refine your ear training. Soon, you'll be navigating the sonic landscape with finesse, crafting music that speaks to your soul and resonates with the world around you.

Pitch and Tone Development for Guitarists

Finding your voice on the guitar is more than mastering chords and strumming patterns. It's a transformative journey, a quest to weave your emotions, personality, and unique musical vision into every note you play. This section is your guide on this path, with tools and techniques to refine your pitch and tone, allowing your guitar to truly sing with your voice.

Rhythm

Strumming isn't only about keeping time. It's about painting dynamic landscapes of rhythm and texture. Explore a world beyond basic down-strums:

- **Alternating Strums:** Compose a medley of rhythm with the classic alternating down-strum and up-strum pattern. Start slow, focusing on accuracy and a smooth transition, then gradually increase your speed as you gain confidence.

- **Ghost Strums:** Add subtle rhythmic accents with ghost strums. Lightly brush your pick across the strings without fully engaging them, creating a percussive and mellow sound, adding depth and intrigue to your playing.

- **Palm Muting:** Tame the natural ring of your strings with palm muting. Rest your palm lightly on the bridge or lower strings while strumming, creating a focused, punchy sound ideal for heavier rhythms and accents.

Fingerpicking

Fingerpicking transforms your guitar into a canvas for intricate melodies and harmonies. Master these techniques to interweave your voice into every note:

- **Fingerstyle Rolls:** Don't merely pick individual notes. Let your fingers dance across the strings in rhythmic patterns like the alternating thumb roll or the Travis picking pattern. These rolls add a mesmerizing layer of texture and movement to your playing.

- **Hybrid Picking:** Combine the power of strumming with the precision of fingerpicking. Alternate between using a pick and your fingers within the same phrase, creating a dynamic and versatile sound that seamlessly blends rhythm and melody.

Embellishments

Go beyond the basics and inject personality into your playing with embellishments:

- **Vibrato:** Add warmth and emotional depth to your notes with a slight wobble in pitch. Experiment with different speeds and intensities to find your signature vibrato style.

- **Bends:** Bend strings to create expressive bluesy phrases and soaring leads. Start with simple half-step bends and gradually explore full-step and beyond as your technique improves.

- **Hammer-ons and Pull-offs:** Add percussive accents and melodic flourishes by fretting notes without picking (hammer-ons) or releasing them without picking (pull-offs). Master these techniques to create smooth, flowing passages showcasing your musicality.

Scales

Scales are the building blocks of music, and diligently practicing them refines your articulation and phrasing. Focus on these essential aspects:

- **Clean Note Transitions:** Ensure smooth, legato transitions between notes. Practice scales slowly and deliberately, focusing on finger placement and picking accuracy.

- **Dynamics and Accents:** Don't be a monotone robot. Vary your picking intensity to add emphasis and emotional nuance to your playing.

- **Phrasing:** Think beyond individual notes and focus on how you connect them into phrases. Experiment with rhythmic groupings and melodic contours to find your unique phrasing style.

Discovering Your Sonic Universe

Finding your voice is a continuous journey of exploration and experimentation. Embrace these tips to unlock your unique musical identity:

- **Record Yourself:** Listen back critically to identify areas for improvement. This self-reflection is crucial to identifying and refining your signature sound.

- **Explore Different Tunings:** Standard tuning is a great starting point, but venturing into alternative tunings like open G or drop D opens new sonic possibilities and inspires creative breakthroughs.

- **Immerse Yourself in Diverse Music:** Listen to a wide range of musical styles and guitarists. From blues to jazz to flamenco, each genre offers unique approaches to pitch and tone that can enrich your playing.

Bonus Tip: Seek a supportive mentor or community. A good teacher or joining a group of fellow guitarists provides invaluable guidance, support, and inspiration on your musical journey. A supportive community creates a space for sharing ideas, collaborating, and learning from each other's experiences. So, whether it's finding a skilled instructor, joining an online forum, or jamming with local musicians, remember that a strong support system will go a long way in helping you find and refine your skills as a guitarist.

As you close the final page of Chapter 3, remember that mastering technique is not an end goal but a gateway. The practiced strokes, the precise finger placement, and the refined sense of pitch are elements that come together to empower you, not restrict you. They are the tools with which you sculpt your musical vision, giving life to melodies that whisper and scream, dance, and flow.

Embrace this newfound vocabulary of playing, experimenting, practicing, and, above all, letting your emotions guide your fingers. Soon, the technical drills will fade into the background, replaced by the pure joy of expressing yourself through the enchanting song of the guitar. Now go forth, armed with your knowledge and passion, and let the music within you take flight.

Chapter 4: Building Guitar Skills

The call of the strings has beckoned you, and you've bravely embarked on this musical adventure. You've mastered the basics, strumming your first chords and plucking out simple melodies. But now the horizon beckons, urging you to climb the next peak of your guitar mastery. This chapter is packed with tools and techniques to transform your fledgling skills into a confident musical voice.

7. *Keep practicing! Source: https://www.pexels.com/photo/girl-playing-guitar-for-her-dad-4815373/*

Prepare to discover the world of strokes and melodies, where you'll refine your strumming patterns, add rhythmic flair with pick strokes, and weave enchanting melodies with your fingers. You'll decipher the secrets of guitar sheet music and notation, transforming those squiggly symbols into a clear roadmap for your musical journey. Finally, you'll equip yourself with the wisdom of effective practice, guiding you in crafting a routine that unlocks your full potential and propels you toward musical excellence.

Learning through Repetition: The Path to Guitar Greatness

The siren song of guitar mastery beckons many. Yet, the journey seems daunting, filled with intricate fingerpicking patterns, lightning-fast solos, and chords that contort your fingers into seemingly impossible shapes. Amid the technical complexities lies a fundamental truth. Repetition is the unsung hero of guitar mastery. While flashy techniques and complex harmonies capture the spotlight, the consistent, dedicated repetition of melodies and strokes lays the foundation for musical fluency and expression. It isn't a monotonous slog but a strategic practice method that unlocks your potential and transforms you from a hesitant strummer to a confident musician.

Deconstructing the Wall: Taming a Beastly Song

Ever stared at a challenging guitar solo, your fingers itching yet intimidated by its seemingly insurmountable complexity? Don't let it overwhelm you. Instead, look at it as a majestic wall, ready to be scaled one brick at a time. Here's your tactical guide:

- **Divide and Conquer:** Listen intently, dissecting the solo into smaller, manageable phrases or licks. Identify those sections that pose the biggest challenge and become your immediate targets.

- **Isolating the Elements:** Treat each identified phrase like a mini-boss battle. Practice it slowly and deliberately, focusing on every detail. Pay close attention to finger placement, picking patterns, and embellishments that add flair. Don't move on until you execute it flawlessly, even with your eyes closed.

- **Connecting the Dots:** Once you've mastered each phrase, it's time to assemble your musical masterpiece. Start by piecing the sections together, gradually increasing the tempo as your confidence grows. Slow and steady wins the race. Rushing will only lead to frustration and hinder your progress.

The Metronome: Your Rhythm-Taming Ally

Timing and rhythm are the lifeblood of a musical performance. They are the invisible threads that weave notes into melody and groove. In this rhythmic quest, the humble metronome becomes your invaluable companion:

- **Start Slow and Steady:** For now, forget about impressing anyone (including yourself) with speed. Set the metronome at a tempo significantly slower than you can handle. It lets you focus on each note and stroke with laser-like precision, ensuring every movement is deliberate and controlled.

- **Gradually Increase the Challenge:** As your accuracy and comfort improve, incrementally increase the metronome's speed. It should be a gentle nudge, pushing you to refine your rhythmic sensibilities and expand your boundaries.

- **Internalize the Pulse:** Don't just listen to the click. Feel it resonate within you. Focus on incorporating the metronome's steady pulse into your playing, allowing it to guide your fingers and pick even when not physically present. This internalization forms the bedrock for consistent and confident playing, regardless of the tempo.

Slow and Deliberate: The Seeds of Mastery

The allure of shredding solos and lightning-fast strumming might be tempting, but slow and deliberate practice is the secret weapon of guitar mastery. Here's why:

- **Isolating the Gremlins:** Slowing down acts like a magnifying glass, revealing even the subtlest technical imperfections and errors in your playing. You address them with focused attention by dissecting them at a snail's pace, eliminating them before they become ingrained habits.

- **Building Muscle Memory:** Repetitions at a slower tempo create neural pathways in your brain, training your fingers and pick to execute techniques smoothly and automatically. It becomes the foundation upon which you gradually build speed and complexity without sacrificing accuracy.

- **Confidence through Precision:** Slow practice fosters control and mastery over your instrument. Your confidence blossoms as you consistently nail each note and stroke at a slower tempo, empowering you to tackle faster passages with newfound assurance. Rushing is the enemy of progress, so take your time, embrace the repetition, and let the seeds of mastery slowly take root.

Remember the transformative power of repetition when you find yourself frustrated by a tricky melody or struggling to keep up with the rhythm. Break down the challenges, embrace the metronome, and practice slowly and deliberately. With dedication and a dash of patience, you'll discover that repetition isn't just a tedious exercise. It's the key that unlocks the door to your guitar mastery, paving the way for a musical journey filled with confidence, expression, and pure joy.

Reading the Script: Unveiling the Secrets of Guitar Sheet Music

Have you gazed at a page of guitar sheet music and wondered at its squiggly lines and symbols resembling an alien language? This seemingly complex script holds the key to a vast musical library, waiting to be unlocked by the power of understanding. It's time for you to uncover notation, decipher the code, and equip yourself with the tools to confidently navigate the pages of your favorite songs.

The Building Blocks: Music Notation 101

8. *Music notation is the language of music. Source: https://pixabay.com/vectors/silhouette-musical-clef-bass-3275055/*

Before diving into the intricacies of guitar sheet music, you must lay the foundation with some basic music notation knowledge:

- **Staff Lines and Spaces:** Notations have a five-line grid, the staff, with four spaces in between. Each line and space represents a different musical pitch, with notes positioned accordingly.

- **Treble Clef:** This curly symbol perched at the beginning of the staff indicates that the notes on the lines represent higher-pitched sounds, typically played by the higher strings on your guitar.

- **Notes and Their Values:** Round ovals represent notes, and their shape determines the duration. A whole note lasts four beats, a half note two beats, and so on. Flags and beams attached to notes further subdivide their duration.

- **Rhythm and Time Signatures:** The time signature at the beginning of the staff tells you how many beats are in each measure and what note gets one beat. A 4/4 time signature means there are four beats per measure, and a quarter note gets one beat.

Tablature: A Visual Guide for Fretboard Navigation

While traditional music notation reigns supreme, some guitarists prefer the simplicity of tablature or tab. These six horizontal lines represent your guitar's strings, with numbers on the lines indicating which fret to press on each string to play a specific note. Here's why a tab can be advantageous:

- **Visually Intuitive:** Tab directly translates notes to fret positions, making it easier for beginners to grasp the physical aspects of playing.

- **Focus on the Fretboard:** The Tab doesn't require understanding traditional notation, allowing you to concentrate on finger placement and technique.

- **Popular Music Friendly:** Many contemporary guitar songs use tab notation, making learning songs from your favorite artists easier.

Sight-Reading: From Deciphering to Playing

The ultimate goal is sight-reading, playing music directly from the page without prior practice. Here are tips to develop this valuable skill:

- **Start Simple:** Begin with easy pieces that use basic rhythms and notes. Gradually increase the difficulty as your skills improve.

- **Practice Regularly:** Dedicate time each day to sight-reading exercises. The more you practice, the faster you'll develop fluency.

- **Sing Along:** Singing the notes as you play reinforces the connection between notation and sound, aiding in memorization and comprehension.

- **Use a Metronome:** Maintain a steady tempo while sight-reading to develop your rhythm and timing.

Sight-reading takes time and dedication. Don't get discouraged if you encounter challenges. Embrace the learning process, celebrate your progress, and keep practicing. Soon, you'll be confidently navigating the pages of your favorite songs, transforming written music into beautiful melodies and captivating rhythms flowing from your fingertips.

Practice Power: Unleashing Your Guitar Potential through Smart Routines

The path to guitar mastery is paved with dedicated practice. However, aimlessly noodling on your strings for hours rarely yields the desired results. To truly unlock your potential, you need a structured practice routine. It's a roadmap guiding your progress, maximizing your time, and fueling your musical journey with focused effort.

Setting Goals: Aiming for the Stars (and Landing on the Fretboard)

Every successful journey starts with a clear destination. In guitar practice, this destination has realistic and achievable goals. Here's how to chart your course:

- **Start Small and Specific:** Don't overwhelm yourself with ambitious goals like "become a guitar virtuoso in a month." Instead, set smaller, attainable targets like "mastering an E major barre chord" or "learning the intro to my favorite song."

- **Focus on Progress, not Perfection:** Everyone makes mistakes, even the shredding masters you admire. Embrace the learning process and focus on incremental improvements. Celebrate the smallest victories- because they are stepping stones on your path to mastery.

- **Create a Timeline:** Don't let your goals float in the nebulous ether. Assign achievable deadlines to each target, creating a sense of urgency and keeping you motivated. A goal without a deadline is just a wish.

Mistake Mission: From Foes to Fuel

Mistakes are inevitable companions on your musical journey. However, instead of seeing them as roadblocks, view them as valuable learning opportunities. Here's how to turn those stumbles into stepping stones:

- **Identify the Enemy:** The first step is recognizing the mistake. Pay close attention to where you falter, be it a missed note, a sloppy transition, or an uneven rhythm. Isolating the problem allows you to address it directly.

- **Slow It Down, Sherlock:** Trying to fix a mistake at full speed is like searching for a dropped contact lens in a sandstorm. Slow down the problematic section to analyze each note and movement with laser-like focus.

- **Practice Makes Perfect:** Once you understand the mistake, repeatedly practice the correct technique. Repetition trains your muscle memory and ensures the correct execution becomes ingrained, pushing the faulty technique into the past.

Finding Your Groove: Practice Methods that Sing to Your Soul

Practice doesn't have to be a monotonous chore. Discover methods that spark your passion and keep you engaged:

- **Jam Along:** Find backing tracks online or jam with friends, letting your creativity flow as you improvise and experiment. Jamming is a fantastic way to develop ear training, rhythmic skills, and overall musicality.

- **Record Yourself:** Capture your playing and listen to the playback critically. This self-assessment reveals areas for improvement and allows you to track your progress, fueling your motivation to keep striving.

- **Make It Fun:** Incorporate elements you enjoy. Learn songs from your favorite genres, practice techniques used by musicians you admire, or even write your music. When you're having fun, practice feels less like work and more like an exciting musical adventure.

Building a successful practice routine is an ongoing process of exploration and adaptation. Experiment, discover what works best for you, and most essentially, enjoy the journey. With dedication, smart practice, and a dash of fun, you'll be amazed at your progress, transforming your guitar playing from a casual pastime into a powerful expression of your musical soul.

As you close this chapter, remember that your guitar journey is merely beginning. The skills you've honed, the techniques you've mastered, and the knowledge you've gleaned are only the first steps on your path to musical mastery. Keep the fire of curiosity alive, embrace the challenges that lie ahead, and, most importantly, never stop playing. Let the music flow from your fingers, let your soul speak through the strings, and forever cherish the joy of creating music with your two hands.

Chapter 5: Playing the Guitar

The calluses have formed, your fingers dance across the fretboard with newfound confidence, and chords flow from your fingertips like cascading melodies. You've mastered the fundamentals, and now, the true adventure begins. This chapter transports you into the heart and soul of guitar playing, equipping you with the techniques and secrets to transform those technical skills into captivating music that resonates with you and your audience.

9. Discover the art of expressive and emotive playing. Source: https://www.pexels.com/photo/boy-playing-an-acoustic-guitar-7520785/.

Forget monotonous repetitions and robotic strumming. You'll explore practice tips and tricks that maximize your time, spark your creativity, and inject your playing with passion. Discover how to easily navigate challenging passages, develop lightning-fast picking skills, and tackle intricate bends and vibrato effects. However, technique is only the foundation. You'll also discover the art of expressive and emotive playing, revealing the secrets to infusing your music with dynamics, phrasing, and soul. Learn how to bend notes with conviction, use vibrato to add depth and drama, and master storytelling through your fingertips.

Beyond the Mechanics: Tips and Tricks for Practice

Sure, mastering the guitar takes dedication. But it's not about mindlessly drilling scales and chords. It's about practicing smart, maximizing your time, and nurturing a love for the instrument that keeps you returning for more. So, ditch the robotic repetitions and explore practice tips and tricks that will transform your guitar journey from a mechanical grind into an engaging, rewarding experience.

Warm Up Like a Pro: Prepare Your Fingers for Flight

Imagine a sprinter launching into a race without stretching. Not pretty, right? The same applies to your guitar playing. Before diving headfirst into complex techniques, warm up your hands and fingers to avoid injury and ensure optimal performance:

- **Gentle Stretches:** Start with simple finger stretches, rotating your wrists and shaking your arms. It'll wake up your muscles and joints, preparing them for the demands of playing.

- **Chromatic Scales:** Play slow, ascending, and descending chromatic scales on each string. It loosens your fingers, improves dexterity, and warms up your fretting hand for the technical challenges ahead.

- **Easy Picking Patterns:** Don't jump straight into shredding. Start with simple picking patterns like alternate picking or fingerpicking exercises to warm up and coordinate your picking hand.

Step Back and Breathe: Avoiding the Fatigue Trap

Have you practiced for hours, feeling increasingly frustrated and seeing no improvement? You've fallen into the fatigue trap. Taking breaks is crucial for maintaining focus and preventing burnout:

- **Set a Timer:** Schedule short breaks every 15-20 minutes, even if it's to stand up, stretch, and grab a glass of water. These mini-pauses refresh your mind and body, allowing you to return to practice with renewed focus and energy.

- **Change Gears:** Don't get stuck in a rut. If you're struggling with a particular technique, switch to something else for a while. Come back to the challenging section with a fresh perspective and renewed energy.

- **Listen to Your Body:** Pay attention to your physical and mental state. Stop and take a longer break if you're tired, frustrated, or sore. Pushing through fatigue leads to bad habits and hinders progress.

Celebrate Your Victories: Tracking Progress for Motivation

Practice is a journey, and like any journey, so celebrating your progress is important. Keeping track of your achievements fuels motivation and reminds you how far you've come:

- **Set Achievable Goals:** Break down your goals into smaller, manageable milestones. Mastering a new chord, nailing a tricky solo, or learning a new song are victories worth celebrating.

- **Keep a Practice Journal:** Document your progress, noting down the techniques you're working on, the challenges you're facing, and your successes. Looking back at your journey will inspire and remind you of your ever-growing skills.

- **Reward Yourself:** Celebrate your milestones with small rewards. Treat yourself to a new pick, a lesson from your favorite guitarist, or take a day off from practice to recharge and enjoy your musical achievements.

Practice is not only about the destination. It's also about the journey. Embrace the process, experiment, have fun, and don't be afraid to make mistakes. With these tips and tricks in your arsenal, you'll transform your guitar practice into a rewarding experience that fuels your passion and propels you toward musical mastery.

Techniques for Expressive Guitar Playing

You've mastered the chords and conquered the scales, and your fingers dance across the fretboard with newfound confidence. However, something's missing. A spark of emotional depth elevates your playing from mere technical proficiency to something exceptionally captivating. The secret is in expressive playing. It's about knitting your emotions into the music, telling a story through each note, and captivating your audience with your unique voice.

Dynamics: The Language of Loud and Soft

When a story is told in a monotone voice, it's not very engaging, right? The same applies to music. Dynamic control, the ability to play both soft (pianissimo) and loud (fortissimo), adds depth and dimension to your playing:

- **Become a Storyteller:** Use dynamics to paint a sonic picture, highlighting the music's emotions. Learn to play the soft, introspective whisper of a secret shared, then the powerful crescendo of a soaring declaration of love. Let the music ebb and flow, mirroring the natural rise and fall of emotions within the song.

- **Embrace the Metronome:** Don't underestimate the power of practice with a metronome. Set it to a slow tempo and focus on playing each note with intention, experimenting with crescendos and decrescendos to build tension and release with control. Learn to sculpt the sound, breathing life into each phrase with the subtle dance of dynamics.

- **Listen and Learn:** Pay attention to how your favorite guitarists use dynamics to shape their music. Analyze their phrasing, articulation, and how they build emotion through volume variations. Transcribe their techniques, experiment with them on your own, and gradually incorporate them into your playing.

Bends, Slides, and Ornaments: Adding Flair to Your Phrasing

Bends, slides, and hammer-ons are the spices that add flavor and personality to your playing:

- **Bends that Sing:** Don't just bend notes. Bend them with conviction, letting them rise and fall like a soulful sigh. Use vibrato at the peak of the bend for added expressiveness, and experiment with different bending speeds to create tension and release, mimicking the nuances of human emotion. Let your fingers become vocal cords, bending each note with the same depth, and feeling you would infuse into your voice.

- **Slides that Speak:** Slides can be smooth and legato, like a gentle caress, or gritty and aggressive, like a burst of anger. Experiment with various slide techniques and lengths to add texture and emotional depth to your phrasing. Let your fingers glide across the fretboard, telling a story through each slide and pitch shift.

- **Hammer-ons and Pull-offs:** These techniques add a percussive flair to your playing and create staccato bursts of energy or smooth legato transitions, injecting rhythm, and texture into your musical tapestry. Your fingers become tiny hammers and drumsticks, tapping, and pulling on the strings, adding a layer of dynamic energy to your music.

Vibrato and Palm Muting: Shaping Your Tone

Vibrato adds a shimmering quality to your notes, while palm muting creates a percussive, muted sound:

- **Vibrato with Purpose:** Use vibrato sparingly and with intention, letting it shimmer on sustained notes like a teardrop glistening in the sunlight. A gentle vibrato adds depth and emotion, while a wider vibrato creates a sense of drama and excitement. Infuse each note with a touch of vulnerability or raw power, depending on the music's emotional context.

- **Palm Muting for Texture:** Palm muting is a versatile technique that adds rhythmic emphasis, creates a funky groove, and a unique texture to your sound. Experiment with different palm muting positions and pressures to explore its sonic possibilities for a layer of rhythmic intrigue or percussive grit to your musical narrative.

Remember, expressive playing is a journey, not a destination. Don't be afraid to experiment, make mistakes, and find your unique voice. With dedication and practice, you'll transform your guitar playing into a powerful tool for emotional expression, captivating your audience and leaving them wanting more. So, pick up your instrument, unleash your emotions, and let your music come alive.

The Soul of Guitar Music: Connecting with Emotion

In its simplest form, the guitar is a collection of wood and strings. However, in the hands of a skilled musician, it becomes a powerful instrument of emotion, a conduit channeling feelings and stories directly to the hearts of listeners. Mastering the technical aspects of playing is crucial, but the ability to connect with emotion truly elevates a guitarist from a skilled technician to a captivating artist.

Understanding the Mood and Message

Every song has a soul, a unique emotional core that the artist pours into their music. Before you even pick up your guitar, take time to understand the song's message:

- **Listen Actively:** Focus on the lyrics, the melody, and the song's atmosphere. What emotions does it evoke? Is it a joyful celebration, a melancholic ballad, or a powerful anthem of defiance?

- **Imagine the Story:** Close your eyes and visualize the scene the song paints. Who are the characters? What are they feeling? Immerse yourself in the emotional landscape of the music, allowing it to resonate within you.

- **Find Your Connection:** Ask yourself how this song connects with your emotions and experiences. Can you relate to the joy, sadness, or anger expressed in the music? Finding a personal connection will fuel your emotional expression when you play.

Dynamics and Phrasing: The Language of Storytelling

Now that you understand the song's soul, it's time to tell its story through your playing. Use dynamics and phrasing to paint a sonic picture, mirroring the emotional arc of the music:

- **Soft Whispers and Powerful Crescendos:** Don't just play the notes at the same volume. Use dynamics to highlight the emotional peaks and valleys of the song. Whisper secrets during quiet passages and unleash your full voice during moments of passion and intensity.

- **Phrasing with Purpose:** Pay attention to how the melody breathes and flows. Use phrasing to create tension and release, mirroring the natural rise and fall of human emotion. Add subtle nuances and variations that breathe life into the music.

- **Silence Is Golden:** Don't be afraid to let the music breathe. Use strategically placed pauses and spaces to create anticipation and emphasize the emotional impact of key phrases. Silence becomes a powerful tool in your storytelling arsenal, adding depth and meaning to your musical narrative.

Infusing Your Voice: Injecting Personality and Emotion

While respecting the song's original message is important, don't be afraid to inject your personality and emotions into your playing. It makes your interpretation unique and captivating:

- **Find Your Voice:** Experiment with different techniques and approaches. How can you use bends, vibrato, and palm muting to express your emotional interpretation of the song?

- **Aim to Improvise:** While staying true to the overall melody and structure, add your embellishments and flourishes. Let your fingers dance and express your unique musicality, adding a layer of personal expression to the song.

- **Play with Conviction:** Believe in what you're playing. Pour your heart and soul into each note, letting your passion and emotions shine. Remember, the audience connects with your authenticity, not only your technical prowess.

As you close this chapter, let the newfound techniques and insights resonate within you. Guitar playing is a lifelong journey, a continuous exploration of expression and self-discovery. Embrace the challenges, cherish the breakthroughs, and never stop playing. Let the music flow from your fingertips, let your soul speak through the strings, and forever revel in the joy of creating music with your two hands.

The greatest guitarists aren't defined by their technical prowess but by their ability to move listeners, evoke emotions, and tell stories through music. With the tools and guidance in this chapter, you're well on your way to crafting your musical narrative, one captivating note at a time. The world awaits your musical masterpiece.

Chapter 6: Guitar Care and Maintenance

Like a cherished friend, your guitar deserves proper care and attention to ensure it stays in top condition, ready to resonate with your music for years. This chapter uncovers the essential guitar care and maintenance practices, equipping you with the knowledge and skills to keep your instrument sounding its best, playing smoothly, and looking its most beautiful.

10. Maintain your guitar. Source: https://www.pexels.com/photo/brown-wooden-chair-beside-guitar-case-6860827/

From proper cleaning and string changes to storage and handling guidelines, you'll explore everything you need to know to nurture your guitar's health and prevent potential problems. You'll tackle common troubleshooting issues, empowering yourself to identify and address minor adjustments. It'll save you time and money while fostering a deeper connection with your musical partner.

The Secrets of Proper Maintenance

Ever strum a chord only to be met with a jarring dissonance? The culprit? Likely an out-of-tune guitar. While regularly tuning your strings is crucial, achieving and maintaining perfect pitch requires more than a trusty tuner. It demands proper maintenance and dedication to keeping your instrument in optimal condition to ensure it sings in perfect harmony with your musical aspirations.

Strings: The Foundation of Perfect Pitch

Old, worn-out strings are dull and lifeless. They're notoriously unstable, prone to snapping, and resistant to staying in tune. Regular string changes are essential for optimal sound and intonation:

- **Frequency Matters:** How often you change strings depends on your playing style and frequency. Heavy players might need new strings every week, while casual strummers can go a month or two. Listen for signs of wear and tear, like dull tone, increased breakage, and tuning instability.

- **Cleaning Routine:** Don't underestimate the power of clean strings. Wipe down your strings after each playing session with a soft cloth to remove dirt and sweat, contributing to tuning instability.

- **Stretching Is Key:** New strings stretch and lose their tuning easily. Before settling into your final tuning, gently stretch each string by pulling it upward from the bridge while holding it down at the nut. Repeat this process a few times until the string holds its tuning.

Truss Rod: Balancing the Neck

The truss rod is a hidden hero, a metal rod inside your guitar's neck that adjusts its curvature. A properly adjusted truss rod ensures the strings have the correct clearance from the fretboard, which is essential for accurate intonation and avoiding buzzing:

- **Signs of Trouble:** If your guitar has excessive fret buzz or the action (distance between strings and fretboard) is too high, your truss rod might need adjustment. Conversely, it might be too tight if the strings are too close to the fretboard or the action is too low.

- **Proceed with Caution:** Adjusting the truss rod requires care and precision. Consult a qualified guitar technician if you're unsure, as improper adjustments will damage your instrument.

- **Small Turns, Big Impact:** When adjusting the truss rod, turn it only slightly (usually 1/4 turn at a time) and wait several minutes before checking the results. The truss rod works slowly, so patience is crucial.

Intonation: Dialing in Perfect Fretting

Intonation is the accuracy of each note played across the fretboard. If your guitar is properly intonated, each fret will play the correct pitch, ensuring your chords and melodies ring true:

- **Tools of the Trade:** You'll need a tuner and a small screwdriver to adjust the intonation screws at the bridge.

- **Fret-by-Fret Check:** Play each string open and then at the 12th fret. Use your tuner to check the pitch at both positions. If the note at the 12th fret is sharp, shorten the string by adjusting the bridge saddle toward the headstock. If it's flat, lengthen the string by moving the saddle away from the headstock.

- **Patience and Precision:** Intonation adjustment requires patience and a keen ear. Fine-tune each string, checking and rechecking until each note rings true across the entire fretboard.

Proper maintenance is an ongoing process, not a one-time fix. By incorporating these practices into your guitar routine, you'll ensure your instrument remains in optimal condition, its strings sing perfectly harmoniously, and your music resonates with the clarity and accuracy it deserves.

Proper Storage and Handling

Your guitar deserves proper care and attention, ensuring it remains safe and sound, ready to resonate with your music for years. Here are essential guitar storage and handling practices

---

to protect your instrument from harm wherever your musical journey takes you.

Choosing the Right Case and Storage Location

Your guitar case is a knight's armor, shielding your instrument from bumps, scratches, and the perils of everyday life. Choosing the proper case and storage location is paramount:

- **Case Considerations:** Opt for a sturdy case that fits your guitar snugly, offering adequate padding and protection. Hard cases offer superior protection but can be bulky, while gig bags are lighter but might not provide the same security. Consider your travel needs and choose accordingly.

- **Location:** Avoid storing your guitar in extreme temperatures or humidity. Damp basements and scorching attics are enemies of wood and strings. Opt for a cool, dry room with consistent temperatures, away from direct sunlight and drafts.

- **Stand Tall (or Lie Down):** If you don't use a case, invest in a sturdy guitar stand that keeps your instrument upright and stable. Avoid hanging your guitar on the wall, as the tension on the neck can cause long-term damage.

Protecting Your Guitar from Environmental Threats

Fluctuations in humidity and temperature wreak havoc on your guitar, causing warping, cracking, and fret sprouts. Here's how to combat these environmental threats:

- **Humidity:** Invest in a humidifier or dehumidifier to maintain optimal humidity levels (around 45-55%) in your storage space. Regularly monitor humidity levels and adjust your humidifier or dehumidifier accordingly.

- **Temperature:** Avoid exposing your guitar to extreme temperatures. Don't leave it in a hot car or under a heating vent. Gradual temperature changes are less harmful, so if you need to take your guitar outside, let it adjust to the new environment slowly.

- **Sunshine:** Keep your guitar away from direct sunlight, which can fade the finish and damage the wood. If storing near a window, use curtains or blinds to block the sun's rays.

Safe Transportation Practices

Taking your guitar on the road is exciting, but it requires careful planning and proper transportation practices:

- **Case Closed:** Always use a sturdy case when traveling, ensuring your guitar is well protected from bumps, jostles, and accidental drops.

- **Extreme Conditions:** Avoid storing your guitar in the trunk of your car, especially during extreme weather conditions. Opt for the passenger compartment or a temperature-controlled storage area.

- **Airline Adventures:** If flying, check your guitar as oversized baggage or carry it on with proper documentation and airline approval. Invest in a sturdy travel case specifically designed for airline travel.

By following these simple yet essential practices, you'll ensure your instrument remains protected from harm. Choose the proper case, store it wisely, protect it from environmental threats, and travel carefully, ensuring your cherished musical companion remains safe and sound.

Troubleshooting Common Guitar Issues Like a Pro

Strumming along only to be met with an unwelcome buzz? Can't seem to hit those high notes without fretting out? Even the most seasoned musicians encounter common issues from time to time. However, this section will equip you with the knowledge and skills to identify and fix minor problems before you throw in the towel.

Diagnosing and Banishing the Unwanted Hum

The pesky buzzing sound on a guitar is a real mood killer. Here's how to identify and address the culprit:

- **String Buzz:** Check for loose strings or uneven string height. Adjust the string action at the bridge or truss rod. Ensure proper string gauge and avoid over-tuning.

- **Fret Buzz:** Identify the problematic frets by playing each note slowly. If the buzz occurs only on certain frets, it might be a high fret issue. Consider minor fret filing or seek professional help for more complex adjustments.

- **Grounding Issues:** Loose electrical connections can cause buzzing in electric guitars. Check the output jack, pickup selector switch, and loose wires for proper grounding.

Conquering the High Notes Confidently

Hitting those high notes without fretting out requires proper technique and a well-maintained instrument. Here's how to tackle this common issue:

- **Action Adjustment:** Ensure the string action is not too high, making pressing down on the frets difficult. Adjust the bridge or truss rod as needed.

- **Fret Wear:** Worn-out frets will cause fretting out, especially on higher notes. Consider a professional fret leveling or crowning if necessary.

- **Technique Matters:** Practice proper fretting technique, ensuring you press the strings down firmly and perpendicular to the fretboard.

Tuning Troubles

Maintaining perfect pitch is an ongoing battle, but understanding common tuning issues will help you win the war:

- **String Quality:** Old, worn-out strings are prone to losing their tuning stability. Invest in quality strings and change them regularly.

- **Stretching Is Key:** New strings stretch and lose their tuning easily. Gently stretch each string before tuning to ensure it holds its pitch.

- **Tuning Pegs:** Loose tuning pegs will cause tuning instability. Tighten them gently or replace them if worn out.

DIY Repairs

While some issues require professional attention, you can tackle minor repairs and adjustments yourself:

- **String Changes and Cleaning:** This is an essential skill every guitarist should master. Keep your strings clean and change them regularly for optimal sound and tuning stability.

- **Adjusting the Truss Rod and Bridge:** With proper guidance and caution, you can make minor adjustments to the truss rod and bridge to fix action issues and improve intonation.

- **Replacing Worn-out Parts:** Knobs, pickguards, and worn-out electronics can be easily replaced with readily available parts.

When to Call in the Pros

While DIY repairs are empowering, there are situations where professional help is crucial:

- **Cracks, Breaks, and Major Structural Damage:** These require a skilled luthier for proper repair and restoration.

- **Electrical Issues:** Complex wiring problems in electric guitars are best left to experienced technicians.

- **Fretwork and Neck Adjustments:** Extensive fretwork, such as leveling or crowning, and delicate neck adjustments require specialized tools and expertise.

Remember, troubleshooting is a skill that develops with experience. Don't be afraid to experiment, learn from your mistakes, and seek professional help when needed. By understanding common issues and equipping yourself with basic repair knowledge, you'll transform from a frustrated musician to a confident guitar hero.

As you close this chapter, remember that caring for your guitar is an ongoing act of love and respect. Like a well-maintained garden flourishes and yields bountiful blooms, a properly cared-for guitar rewards you with its vibrant sound, smooth playability, and enduring beauty. Embrace the simple yet essential practices outlined in these pages, and you'll prolong the lifespan of your instrument and deepen your connection with your musical companion.

Chapter 7: Exploring Guitar History and Repertoire

The guitar's melody is integrated into human history, echoing across continents and cultures. Its sound has been a soundtrack to revolutions, fueled artistic movements, and provided solace to countless souls. In this chapter, you'll explore the guitar's rich past, present, and future. You'll discover its fascinating cultural and historical context, meet the legendary players who have shaped its sound, and discover the innovative spirit that propels this versatile instrument forward.

11. Explore the guitar's rich past. Source: Nikolai Nevrev, Public domain, via Wikimedia Commons. https://commons.wikimedia.org/wiki/File:A_Guitar_Player_by_ Nikolai_Nevrev,_Murmansk_Regional_Museum_of_Art.JPG

The Guitar's Journey through Culture and History

With its resonant melodies and versatile voice, the guitar has captivated hearts and strummed its way into cultures worldwide. But where did this ubiquitous instrument begin, and how did it evolve into the diverse and beloved musical companion it is today? Buckle up as you venture on a historical and cultural odyssey, tracing the guitar's fascinating journey from humble beginnings to global phenomenon.

From Renaissance Roots to Global Resonance

The guitar's ancestry can be traced to medieval Europe, where instruments like the lute and vihuela laid the groundwork for its development. By the 16th century, the guitar, as you know it, emerged in Spain, with its popularity blossoming across Europe in the following centuries. However, its journey didn't stop there:

- **Transatlantic Travels:** European explorers and colonists carried the guitar across the Atlantic, introducing it to the Americas. Here, it seamlessly blended with indigenous musical traditions, giving rise to unique styles like flamenco in Spain and mariachi in Mexico.

- **African Rhythms and Bluesy Melodies:** The arrival of enslaved Africans in the Americas brought their rich musical heritage, including intricate drumming patterns and soulful vocals. This fusion with the European guitar gave birth to the blues, a genre that later influenced rock and roll and countless other musical styles.

- **Eastern Echoes:** The guitar also journeyed eastward, reaching Asia through trade routes and cultural exchanges. The guitar was adapted to local musical sensibilities in countries like India and Japan, creating unique sounds and playing techniques.

Culture, Migrations, and Technology: Shaping the Guitar's Sound

The guitar's evolution was driven by geography and profoundly shaped by:

- **Cultural Influences:** Each culture infused the guitar with a unique spirit and expression. From the flamenco's fiery passion to the blues' soulful lament, the guitar became a canvas for cultural storytelling.

- **Migrations and Diasporas:** The movement of people across continents led to the cross-pollination of musical styles, further enriching the guitar's repertoire. For instance, the migration of African Americans to urban centers in the United States was crucial in the development of jazz and rock and roll.

- **Technological Advancements:** The invention of new technologies, like the electric guitar and amplification, opened new sonic possibilities, forever changing how the guitar was played and perceived.

The Guitar's Role in Social Movements

The guitar's impact extends far beyond the realm of music. It has been a powerful tool for:

- **Social Commentary and Protest:** From folk singers like Bob Dylan using their guitars to voice dissent against war to Latin American nueva canción artists advocating for social justice, the guitar has been a powerful tool for social commentary and change.

- **Cultural Revolutions:** The guitar played a pivotal role in cultural revolutions like the 1960s counterculture movement in the United States, where artists like Jimi Hendrix and Janis Joplin used their music to challenge societal norms and advocate for peace and love.

- **Unifying Communities:** The guitar's ability to transcend cultural barriers and unite people has made it a powerful tool for fostering community and understanding. From campfire singalongs to global music festivals, the guitar has the power to unite people through music's universal language.

The guitar's journey is a testament to its remarkable adaptability and enduring appeal. From its humble origins to its global presence, the guitar has served as a mirror to cultures, struggles, and triumphs.

Legends of the Six Strings: Iconic Players and Compositions

With its six strings and endless potential, the guitar has birthed countless legends, each leaving an indelible mark on the landscape of music. From bluesy cries to soaring classical melodies, the guitar's versatility has provided a canvas for musical giants to paint their masterpieces. It's time to meet some of these iconic players and discover their groundbreaking compositions, exploring how they shaped the instrument's evolution and the music you love.

Masters of Their Genres

Every genre boasts its pantheon of guitar heroes, each with a distinct voice and style:

- **Blues: Robert Johnson:** Nicknamed the "King of the Delta Blues," Johnson's raw and emotional playing, exemplified in songs like "Cross Road Blues," laid the foundation for generations of blues and rock guitarists.

- **Rock: Jimi Hendrix:** A true guitar innovator, Hendrix redefined the instrument's possibilities using feedback, distortion, and unconventional techniques. His psychedelic masterpiece "Purple Haze" remains a testament to his groundbreaking talent.

- **Classical: Andrés Segovia:** A classical guitar pioneer, Segovia elevated the instrument's status through his virtuosity and dedication to repertoire expansion. His mesmerizing rendition of "Asturias" by Isaac Albéniz is a masterclass in classical guitar artistry.

Compositions That Transcended Genres

Beyond individual players, certain guitar compositions have transcended genres, becoming cultural touchstones:

- **Stairway to Heaven (Led Zeppelin):** Jimmy Page's iconic masterpiece, with its intricate guitar work and soaring melodies, continues to captivate audiences and inspire countless aspiring guitarists.

- **Black Dog (Led Zeppelin):** John Bonham's thunderous drumming and Jimmy Page's heavy guitar riffs in "Black Dog" laid the groundwork for hard rock and heavy metal, forever changing the sonic landscape.

- **Hotel California (Eagles):** Don Felder and Joe Walsh's intertwined guitar lines in "Hotel

California" are a masterclass in melodic interplay, creating an unforgettable soundscape that has resonated for decades.

Evolution in Six Strings

The constant evolution of playing styles and techniques has marked the guitar's journey:

- **From Fingerpicking to Electric Experimentation:** The transition from the fingerpicking styles of blues pioneers like Robert Johnson to the electric pyrotechnics of Jimi Hendrix reflects the ever-expanding sonic possibilities explored by guitarists.

- **From Classical Precision to Rock and Roll Swagger:** The shift from the precise and controlled playing of Andrés Segovia to the loose and energetic style of Chuck Berry showcases the diverse ways the guitar can be approached and mastered.

- **From Blues Bends to Shredding Solos:** The evolution of guitar techniques, from the soulful bends of B.B. King to the shredding acrobatics of Yngwie Malmsteen, demonstrates the instrument's limitless potential for expression and innovation.

The legends of the six strings are more than skilled musicians. They are storytellers, innovators, and cultural icons who have shaped the way you listen to and experience music. By exploring their stories, compositions, and playing styles, you gain a deeper appreciation for the guitar's rich history and enduring influence on the world.

The Guitar's Electric Evolution in the Modern Age

The guitar has always been an instrument of innovation and evolution. Its journey has been marked by a constant push to expand its sonic palette and expressive potential from its humble beginnings to its electrifying presence on the modern stage. It's time to uncover the modern landscape of the guitar, exploring the impact of technology, the rise of new playing styles, and the inspiring individuals who continue to push the boundaries of this ever-evolving instrument.

Technology's Transformative Touch

Technology has become an inseparable companion in the guitar's modern journey:

- **Synthesizers and Samplers:** From the otherworldly textures of Andy Summers' work with The Police to the ambient soundscapes of Steve Vai, guitarists have embraced synthesizers and samplers, expanding their sonic vocabulary beyond the traditional six strings.

- **Effects Pedals:** The humble stomp box has become a guitarist's playground, offering a universe of sonic manipulation from distortion and delay to modulation and fuzz. Effects pedals have become essential tools for shaping a guitarist's unique sound, from the bluesy growl of Eric Clapton's wah-wah to the spacey textures of Radiohead's Jonny Greenwood.

- **Digital Modeling:** Amp modeling and digital effects processors allow guitarists to emulate the sounds of legendary amps and effects within a single compact unit. This versatility has opened up new creative possibilities for players on the go.

The Rise of New Playing Styles and Genres

The boundaries between genres are blurring more than ever, giving rise to exciting new playing styles:

- **Djent and Progressive Metal:** Characterized by complex rhythms, intricate fingerpicking techniques, and heavily distorted tones, djent and progressive metal push the boundaries of technical proficiency and sonic experimentation. Guitarists like Misha Mansoor and Tosin Abasi are at the forefront of this movement.

- **Math Rock and Post-Rock:** Using unconventional time signatures and intricate arrangements, math rock and post-rock guitarists like Steve Morse and Robert Fripp challenge traditional song structures and create cerebral and emotionally resonant soundscapes.

- **Genre-Bending Virtuosos:** Guitarists like St. Vincent and John Mayer seamlessly blend elements of rock, jazz, pop, and blues, creating music that defies categorization and showcases their remarkable versatility.

Modern Masters

Countless contemporary guitarists carry the torch of innovation and inspiration:

- **Nita Strauss:** Shredding stereotypes and preconceived notions about female guitarists, Nita Strauss is a technical powerhouse who seamlessly blends shredding acrobatics with melodic sensibility.

- **Mark Knopfler:** A master of fingerpicking and storytelling, Mark Knopfler's evocative style and timeless compositions continue to inspire generations of guitarists.

- **Derek Trucks:** Steeped in the blues tradition yet constantly pushing boundaries, Derek Trucks' slide guitar mastery and soulful vocals create an unforgettable musical experience.

The guitar's evolution is far from over. With technology providing new tools and adventurous players constantly exploring uncharted sonic territories, the future of the Six Strings is brimming with possibilities.

As you conclude your exploration of the guitar's history and repertoire, it's apparent that this instrument is much more than just six strings and a wooden body. It's a cultural touchstone and a constant source of innovation. The guitar transcends generations and genres from its humble beginnings to its modern-day virtuosity.

Conclusion

Congratulations on reaching the end of your guitar adventure. Throughout these chapters, you've explored the wonderful world of the guitar, from choosing your first instrument and learning basic playing techniques to building your skills and discovering this beloved instrument's rich history and diverse repertoire. It's time to recap the key takeaways from the chapters and celebrate your progress:

Key Takeaways

- **Demystifying the Guitar:** You've learned about the different guitars, their anatomy, and how to choose the right instrument for your size and preferences.

- **Unveiling the Basics:** You've mastered the fundamentals of guitar playing, from holding the instrument and tuning the strings to strumming chords and playing simple melodies.

- **Technique Toolbox:** You've unlocked a treasure trove of playing techniques, including fingerpicking, using a pick, and exploring different chord shapes and progressions.

- **Building Your Skills:** You've learned valuable practice strategies to improve your dexterity, develop your ear, and gain confidence as a player.

- **Unleashing Your Musical Voice:** You've discovered the joy of playing songs you love, from strumming along to your favorite tunes to crafting your musical creations.

- **Guitar Care and Maintenance:** You've learned the importance of proper care to keep your instrument sounding its best and lasting for years.

- **A Journey through Time:** You've explored the rich history of the guitar and its role in various musical genres, gaining a deeper appreciation for this timeless instrument.

Mastering the guitar takes dedication and practice, but most importantly, it's about having fun and expressing yourself through music. Don't be discouraged by challenges. Embrace them as opportunities to learn and grow.

Please take a moment to leave a review for "Guitar for Kids." Your feedback will help improve this guide and inspire future young musicians. Share your thoughts on what you enjoyed most, what you found helpful, and suggestions for future editions. Keep practicing, keep exploring, and keep the music flowing.

References

Campbell, D. (2017, June 23). Learning the Fretboard. Beginner Guitar Lessons. https://beginnerguitarlessons.com/learning-the-fretboard/

Editor, S. (2017, February 10). Guitar Basics - 10 Essential Tips for Beginners. National Guitar Academy. https://nationalguitaracademy.com/guitar-basics/

G, B. (n.d.). Guitar Basics for Beginners. Instructables. https://www.instructables.com/Guitar-Basics-For-Beginners/

MetronomeOnline.com. (2012, December 19). A Checklist of Things Every Guitarist Needs to Learn. Metronome Online. https://www.metronomeonline.com/checklist-guitarist-learn/

Play, F. (n.d.). How to Play Guitar | Learn the Basics of Playing Guitar | Fender. Www.fender.com. https://www.fender.com/pages/how-to-play-guitar

Reo. (2019). How to Play Guitar - Your First Guitar Lesson. Guitarlessons.com. https://www.guitarlessons.com/guitar-lessons/guitar-lessons-for-beginners/first-guitar-lesson

simplifyingtheory.com. (n.d.). Learn How to Play the Guitar in 10 Steps (for beginners) | Simplifying Theory. Https://Www.simplifyingtheory.com/.

https://www.simplifyingtheory.com/learn-how-to-play-the-guitar-lesson-for-beginners/

Thür, C. (2022, May 5). How to Play Guitar | Learn to Play in 12 Steps. Yousician. https://yousician.com/blog/how-to-play-guitar

Wong, C. (2024, January 16). First Guitar Lesson for Beginners - Learn the Basics - Pickup Music. Www.pickupmusic.com. https://www.pickupmusic.com/blog/first-guitar-lesson-for-beginners-learn-the-basics

Made in the USA
Las Vegas, NV
13 December 2024

14052956R00049